Illuminating

Verse

Laurie Wilkinson
The Psychy Poet

'Laurie gives us his take on life; real life observations in verse that everyone can relate to'

Introduction

Oh, and gracious me, another book! My twelfth published in just under nine years, so still going well I think.

As my regular readers will know, books ten and eleven were slightly different in that book ten was a compilation of the best of my humorous poems, (Laurie's Bundle of Poetic Humour) and book eleven was a tribute to my created teddy bears Ted and Beth, (Tea for Two - Poetic Antics of Ted and Beth), which includes some about the animal friends they share my home with. It goes without saying that Ted & Beth have new poems in this book too. But now some details about this new offering.

We're back with my usual pattern of four sections of romance, humour, reflection and tragedy. Included here are the stories behind four of the poems, one from each section, which has proved very popular in my previous books. Also back this time, some limericks are featured (after an absence in book 9).

Sylvie Blackmore, a presenter on BBC Radio Sussex and Surrey, has two poems about her in the book. They stem from me being a guest on her Sunday afternoon show twenty plus times over nearly 3 years. Another presented poem, "Inner Tears" won a prestigious festival poetry competition in 2022. Very topically there are also 3 poems about the NHS and my recent experience of being in hospital for the very first time ever!

In book eight I mentioned milestones and I still continue with this and present this latest book as one of them.

To clarify, my milestones, or achievements, are wonderful compliments given to me, my own feelings, great reviews and an increased awareness of my work on several media settings. This has involved having my poems published recently in two mainstream newspapers, read out and complimented about on national radio and regularly requested to be read at many prestigious events. This has also been compounded with further recognition and success which has all gone beyond my early wildest dreams.

I feel this demonstrates the reasons for my increased confidence in this book, and obviously further promotes awareness and funds for the charity Help for Heroes that I have donated to and supported from the start.

I now leave YOU to explore and find my usual multitudes of brand-new poems, a smattering of popular poems from all of my now eleven previous books, and some new and topical themes. It's a celebration and demonstration of my growing poetic attributes and prolific poem production that I once more have the pleasure of bringing to you.

To help you with some background and further understanding, please be aided by my comprehensive Appendix section which explains some not so obvious poems. I am confident that many of them will touch and resonate with you in some way as we ride the roller coaster of life together.

As ever, please enjoy this my twelfth and latest book as "The Journey Continues".....

Laurie Wilkinson Bsc (hons) RMN

Acknowledgements

I need to state that as this is now my twelfth book and thus the 12th Acknowledgements I have written. I am looking back over the history of all my books to recognise the "help and support" I have had which seems to fall into two main forms. One, the general advice, help, and encouragement to actually write, and Two, the support, assistance and opportunities to promote and sell my books that donate to the excellent charity Help for Heroes that cares for our war wounded and beyond.

The lists of all the people involved in the two points above could be almost endless, so I will just loosely touch upon key players and organisations here, and thank the many others personally. Obviously, over my nearly nine years now of publication, some folks have "come and gone" in the natural movements, involvements and flow of life.

So here we go:

Encouraging and advising on my writing have been my (now late) wife Iris, and all my family. Elizabeth Wright (The Writer) who mentored and advised me from my very start and is currently working on my life story.

Alongside my (often manic) efforts to promote me and my books have been the wonderful Lyn Parsons of National Magic FM Radio with her endorsements, readings and mentions of me. The lovely Sylvie Blackmore of BBC Radio Sussex & Surrey who has now had me as guest on her show multiple times to read my poems and talk about my poetry world, and Simon Herbert of Hailsham FM for my regular guest slots.

The 42nd Highland Regiment (1815) for support and buying my books. Hailsham Chamber of Commerce, The Sussex Newspaper Online for allowing my monthly column for over eight years now. Seb and Team at Tesco Langley for supporting and helping my book sales and collecting for Help for Heroes.

Local East Sussex businesses, shops, pubs, (many who sell my books particularly now Cafe Old Town Eastbourne). The charities and all the wonderful people I meet and liaise with too numerous to mention individually by name. I am particularly grateful to Lesley A T, a colleague from the past, Richard Williams for his advice, Geoff H & Bob "Donbo" long ago school friends, Julie A V, Kelly Brown and family, Debbie & Sharon B's my lead Quality Assurance readers. Many, many more must remain unmentioned but not forgotten as you will be thanked elsewhere and perhaps personally.

Obviously, I must mention James Harvey my excellent Website Guru who has also published this book for me under Bad Goose Publishing as he did my previous four books too. A big thanks to him for all his help, guidance and our new ideas as I strive to continue an increasingly prolific, determined, and hopefully innovative life as a poet and author!

As always, my final recognition of gratitude is to you for taking the time to read this book, and with an even bigger thanks to the kind folks who have bought my previous books, and buy this one too, which as ever ensures my donation to the excellent charity Help for Heroes from all my sales.

Thanks again, and bless you all,

Laurie

A Rouse of Verse

Words and verse can stir emotions
And arouse in many ways,
To makes us more aware of life
And illuminates our days.

For feeling really alive in mind
May give great appreciation,
Of vibes and all the sights we see
Rather than just a bland fixation.

So enjoy what those emotions bring
To make us love and thrive,
Because if you're unaware of this
You cannot be truly alive.

Contents

Laurie Wilkinson

ROMANCE

Laurie Wilkinson

If You See a Chance

A fleeting shadow masked the glance
That was doubtless meant for me,
Although only allowing slight vision
In a half light so that I couldn't see,
Exactly the manner of the look
And how much it was trying to say,
For passing heartbeats can confuse
In what directions best decisions lay.

Because I mostly react spontaneously
And often had been lured into mishaps,
Which although also had brought joy
I should have just walked on perhaps,
But on such quick ideas and dreams
Life can change like the swing of a gate,
And we've heard about hesitations loss
With ponderous actions being too late.

And so with this in mind I turned to face
The lady now looking in my direction,
And was left pitifully gasping for breath
Gazing at such a beautiful perfection,
Or was this just another trick of nature
To encourage us to take a chance?
Maybe like I was clearly doing now,
As I responded to her initial glance.

For I believe in nearly always following
My first suggested or hopeful thought,
To do something rather than have regrets
Of possibilities that failed to be caught,
In our net of love, laughs and desires,
For when older we may sadly recall,
How our inaction caused a torment
Of loss, when we could have had it all.

So reacting in a kind of dreamy stupor
I moved towards this siren-like muse,
With nerve endings screaming loudly
I wondered would I now win or lose?

--ooOoo--

Gift Wrapped

A word, a gift or even just a look
Can lift a heart up to the moon,
And if leading to a romantic love trip
It can't ever arrive for you too soon.
For in a world that has many troubles
We need one special person who cares,
To listen, protect and share your fears
Should life catch you out unawares.

Because now in difficult, complex times
Doing everyday things has become tough,
So someone standing by you helping out
Gives strength if you have had enough
Of taking on the world and battling alone,
For two heads, or more likely two hearts
Are far better than only a solitary one,
With great support to make new starts.

Thus should you find that special person
Who thinks that you are their everything,
Please indulge this precious gift of love
Which can make hearts soar and sing.

So you will feel a very unique person
Although each and every one of us are,
But beside your own muse and soulmate
You'll share great love and happily go far
Along your road, but no longer all alone,
With a personal spirit watching over you
To protect you and send words of love,
Every day and night whatever you do.

--ooOoo--

Snuggle

To snuggle is a really lovely sensation
Like pups or kittens to their mother,
For if you're feeling loved or close
There isn't much better or any other,
Cosiness of a protected satisfaction
That can take stress and fears away,
As letting yourself melt into someone
Will bring a contented, happy day.

So don't become shy or awkward
When you've found someone to love,
And sample simple pleasures of life
Snuggling together just like a glove.
Or possibly squashing up tightly
Knowing it's a joint intimate space,
As you make your sensual moves
Without any thoughts of disgrace.

For our own special moments in life
Are something we have to treasure,
Because a close contentment shared
Doesn't have much greater pleasure.

So I've always tried to practice this
Although at times it comes and goes,
Making us welcome any new return
To tempt snuggles without clothes,
With a happily agreed mutual need
Leading to ecstatic levels of desire.
So snuggle up, love and get taken
To feel a heavenly passions fire.

Because any casual or normal day
When you enjoy cuddling up tight,
Can be a simple life fact for us all
That it's better to snuggle than fight.

--ooOoo--

Catch and Carry

Many of us will at some time
Have challenging periods in life,
Mostly more than the unpleasant
Who seem to have less strife.

But when we're struggling on
There's a lover or caring friend,
Who will be there to help you
And see you get to the end.

For a problem shared it's said
Is a concern halved for you,
But a special person does more
To listen and protect you too.

So is around if you finally fall,
Then will catch you quite secure
Because they are your safety net
And reliable for certain sure.

Thus now is your constant friend
So will lift you up if feeling low,
And catch and carry you safely
To just where you want to go.

--ooOoo--

Beam of Love

In the darkness now I think of you
Though you may be near or far.
And if I saw you would I know,
If you're my missing star?

For it is very hard to find someone
If you don't know how they look.
For I have never seen or met you,
Or found a description in a book.

So maybe that's why in the dark
I fantasise I feel your breath,
Because I'm denied sight or sound
Thus think you're a gift from death.

Though you are not here to touch
And however hard I try to see,
I know you, my mysterious spirit,
Are watching and waiting for me.

In the darkness now I think of you
Though you may be near or far.
So if I saw you how would I know,
If you're my missing star?

Why do I feel your shadowy form
As if you are all around my bed?
So where have you come from,
    To be inside my head?

Thus I'm making a request to meet
    Whatever time, or in a dream.
Perhaps you'll come and take me
To love by the moon's night beam.

For now I know what the truth is,
You're a figment of imagined love,
Someone I met, though didn't see
Who'll be there in the stars above!

--ooOoo--

Echo

Into your wilderness comes a voice
As sweet as any blessed angel singing,
For although unexpected and obscure
It means another human is bringing,
A communication to you from afar
Or possibly close as you can't be sure,
The whereabouts of this vocal wonder
Now breaking the silence you endure.

Although silence can at times be sweet
To bring you a solitary, personal joy,
But other times compounds loneliness
Like being locked out behind a door,
Which seems to prohibit your entry
To pleasures you seem to be missing.
Leaving you feeling totally isolated
From ecstasies of loving and kissing.

So when you hear a voice just for you
All the sad uncertainties will leave,
Giving you joy of a new belonging
With the owners calling you receive,
That now requires a girding of loins
And to prepare taking on all it needs
To leave a solitary confinement now
For special love you want to proceed.

So willingly and minus doubt or question
You go where you are lovingly now led,
Because sadness and empty surroundings
Are swapped for love and joy instead.
But you may wonder who has called you
And turned lonely misery to joy and glee?
Though no great surprising wonder really,
Just a love returned back to you or me.

--ooOoo--

Love and Trees (Story)

The story behind this poem is initially quite a simple one, but then it gets deeper. It also perhaps gives a glimpse of what an old romantic I am, but you decide.

The lead line is based on one of my favourite romance songs, "Here Is Your Paradise" by Chris De Burgh, and my theme is that many people do not know how much they have until it is gone. Of course, love is included in this, and then I go to ally it to the magnificence of trees that are so often taken for granted or not noticed at all?

Clearly then a love is laid out as a gift, but like the trees will it largely go unnoticed or missed until it is too late, and maybe then be mourned if it is lost? Possibly this may strike a distant or more recent chord with you? I sincerely hope you didn't lose out.

Love and Trees

Maybe you'll never see how much I love you
Or possibly realise that you're so adored,
Because it may have all overpowered you
Making you complacent and perhaps bored.
For sometimes too much of a good thing
Can confuse and just seem like the norm,
But do not dismiss all that you receive
Freely given in every way and form.

Perhaps you take the trees for granted
With their magnificent spread and shade,
Forever constant in this glory of gifts
As if by angels they were all made.
For on many occasions in busy lives
Such statuesque wonder isn't seen,
Until arrival of sad or tranquil times
Awakens you to this sea of green.

Standing proudly tall or stretching wide
Poplars, willow, birch or imperial oak,
Nobly constant with liberal generosity
Of beautiful sights that they provoke,
In redundant minds and sad emotions
Confined to the mundane, or dire.
Before unleashing spectacles of delight
Causing a heart to soar much higher.

So the wonders now unseen or noted
Of unconditional love and adoration,
Could easily slip by sadly missed
If not aroused to an ecstatic elation.
Thus take a brief considering moment
And open your beautiful eyes to see,
How this priceless love is passing by
Offered wholly to you from me.

--ooOoo--

Knit Together

A special person is nice to wake up to
Maybe even if they are not right there,
Actually with you at that very moment
It is still wonderful to know they care,
And are thinking of you just the same
When loving thoughts cross the miles,
Because shared feelings with another
Can knit together any opposing styles.

Well that's as long as there are not many
Differing opinions or desired dreams,
Because love can play confusing tricks
So that everything is not as it seems.
Although it is probably true as well
That any opposites can come together,
For a successfully long relationship
Which may be quite hard to untether.

But back to our own far-away muse
Who can call or arrive at any time,
To give you sweet love and adoration
Making you feel special and sublime.
Despite there being no recipe for this
And sometimes taking a while to cook,
For all the very best meals and menu
Are not always exactly as they look.

Thus the very unusual and unexpected
Can add great flavour and tastes too,
Which appears is the case quite often
And I suspect is just like me and you,
When we discuss and deeply share
Ideas, feelings and precise emotions,
As some considerations and joy are felt
Even if separated by miles or oceans.

So hang onto that incredible awareness
That when not in a crowd or are alone,
You have a shadow looking out for you
And realise how together you've grown.

--ooOoo--

Gina Giraffe

This is introducing Gina the genial giraffe
And she has her baby with her as well,
Thus is a very cute and lovely sight
Which may make hearts skip or swell.
Because it is so nice to see cuddly toys
Portrayed as if they were actually real,
Well that is exactly my appreciation
And I love just how they look and feel.

Now giraffes are quite elegant creatures
Slowly moving around to get their food,
Mostly from quite tall trees and branches
Where their height allows them to intrude.
But surprisingly they can also run very fast
With speeds reaching thirty miles an hour,
For although quite spindly and ungainly
Their long legs give great speed and power.

Though not now for our Gina the giraffe
All this ferreting in a hard and busy life,
Because being a lovely soft cuddly toy
She and her infant are free from strife,
As they share space with all the other
Teddy bear friends and animal breeds,
Since I brought her back home with me
To share with others her love and needs.

So like most of the teddies and animal gang
They will come with me to gigs a nice sight,
Appreciated by my audiences who see them
Hearing their poems too, for great delight.

--ooOoo--

Duvet

Snuggling under a duvet is a life joy
Or it can actually be bed covers too,
But however you want to use your bed
The feeling is wonderful for me and you,
Because some see it as just relaxing
Others it's purely for a good night sleep,
Though for some it's a mixture of both
If they conjure up pleasures deep.

For like so many things in our lives
They're often improved or made better,
By sharing them with another person
Who may comfort or loosen the fetter,
That possible restricts or contains you
From those feelings in life you desire.
So may be achieved under the duvet,
When many nice ideas might aspire,

Thus our duvet or bedclothes covering
Can protect us from a deepest dread,
That from our childhood we have learnt
We can do by just covering our head,
And pretending we're in a defensive shell
That nothing can breach or penetrate,
As we cower safely in our sanctuary
Giving succour whatever our state.

But of course the main attraction for many
Is to share this intimate nest with another,
And without doubt the real joy of sharing
Comes to fruition with a special lover,
Who arouses and caresses your passions
That come with body-to-body connection,
Which has delighted both men and women,
From back in history with no correction.

Thus enjoy the duvet refuge how you will
And indulge whatever reactions it breeds,
For we are all so very different at times
So enjoy and satisfy personal needs.

--ooOoo--

Headlight

I have observed you much of late
You may have felt my looking stare,
Perhaps you knew the reason why
Or merely how you seemed to care.

Whilst others queued to build my load
You saw that I walked a lonely road,
And rejection can taste an acid pill
That even survivors blood will spill.
So when light invades consuming dark
Flames can rise from a smallest spark!

--ooOoo--

Love's Recollections

There are many love songs played
And we hear them over and over again,
But although this can seem too much
We all still join in with the refrain.

For nearly everyone at some time
Will have an intensive love interest,
That whilst at times causes heartache
Most people still think it is the best,
Simple but so very special sensation
With someone you care deeply for.
And hearing that they love you too
Makes you need and crave for more.

But soon you may begin to understand
Why all the love songs mean so much,
For whether it causes pain or sweet joy
We cannot resist loves soft touch.

Thus indulge all those fluttering feelings
Coursing rapidly about body and heart,
As you will never forget this occasion
Even if you are trying for a new start.
Because there may often be an overlap
Of a past love's memory calling you.
And while this is not always welcome
There is rarely much you can do.

So now possibly you may have learnt
About love and all that it has to give,
But perhaps like that old sixties song
Its best to love the one you are with.
For they will have great appreciation
On being shown how much you care.
So just try to ignore the recollections
And love this one who is now there.

--ooOoo--

Trinket

A trinket is an ornament or memento
That is of little value and worth.
But could possibly get sentimental
If allied to a special birth,
Or something that's held dear
Becoming an intrinsic part of you.
But mostly the trinket is worthless
Whatever you feel or do.

So why then do we collect them?
When not wanted until seen,
With the initial attraction to them
That soon made us very keen,
To get and own these items
Which we succumbed to and bought,
Though now lay about forgotten
Without a second thought.

Because far more important in life
Are the lovely people there,
With you to make those memories
And wonderful days you share.
So when without a thought or plan
A chance meeting turns to bliss,
That without a shadow of doubt
You wouldn't want to miss.

So going back to our trinkets
And maybe other things we get,
Which cannot hold a candle
To that someone special met.

Who fills our life with sunshine
Even when it's a cloudy day.
For a person to love and treasure
Is a far better gift and way,
To find life's joys and wonder
That a trinket could never do,
As the simple fact of the matter
Is that love is best for you!

--ooOoo--

Loose Connection

It's said there's someone for everybody
And so nobody should be alone,
But this doesn't always come easy
If it seems your intended has flown,
Or has gone right out of your world
To be absent from your sight,
Leaving you all sad and lonely
With no love partner at night.

So the longer that people are left
Without their special person to care,
They may become cynically doubting
Anyone will be theirs to share.
Which can then make them desperate
Or possibly frustrated and grim,
That can come across as unattractive
And put off any future her or him.

But it was all so easy years ago
When young and without much fear,
So laughing and chatting was easy
To anyone who just came near.
Well that was the common myth
But actually only right for a few,
As loves highway is very difficult
Whatever you might try or do.

So let's review this tricky situation
With people who've not found love,
Or maybe was only sad and fleeting
And not becoming a turtle dove.
Thus began a hum drum way of life
Maybe staying with mum and dad,
That can very often be restricting
And no love life found or had.

--ooOoo--

Singing Me Home

The sun was fading as I left my club
And began my slow walk back home,
So I was delighted to be accompanied
By a bird's chorus and so was not alone,
For one little chap and a couple more
Of his very cheerful feathered friends,
Brightened up the darkening evening
With an appreciation that never ends.

So I continued on my merry way
Walking through the tidy little estates,
As my now following little bird friend
Serenaded me alone, or with his mates,
For this happy chorus was not quiet
And made a very happy song to me,
Because sometimes a silence isn't nice
And can be an isolating decree.

For I must say that I had clearly noticed
When I stepped out from my jolly club,
That beginning to walk back on my own
A presiding quiet replaced the noisy hub.

For I had been a part of that joviality
As we all like to both laugh and joke,
So we must be guarded and also aware
That alone silences can prevail to choke,
Happily shared jest and conversations
Making you listen to your head and heart.
Thus I was grateful for the birds singing
And how it had cheered me from the start,
With their great chirping choir full of life
From glorious songsters I couldn't see.
But without doubt they cheered the world
And on being alone, even more for me.

--ooOoo--

HUMOUR

Laurie Two Phones

I'm a far better poet than at techno
But in truth I don't need to be that good,
For although I seem to do reasonably well
Some technological bits aren't understood.
Though lots of people at my age group
Or even younger to be brutally true,
Won't even try to embrace advancements
And many don't have the slightest clue.

However, I had quite a shock recently
When I dared to change my mobile phone,
For a model with a much larger screen
Though soon wished I had left well alone,
Because unknown to my techno innocence
I crossed the phone worlds great divide,
From my apparently simple Apple "iPhone"
To an Android with no place to hide.

So whilst my straightforward little phone
Only seemed to have one task to achieve,
Any goal that I wished to succeed with now
My complex new one caused me to grieve.

Because my non-advert previous phone
Was not an involved complicated device,
Like my new larger and many facet model
Now making me wish I had thought twice,
Before making a leap to more complications
Of my newly purchased mini-computer,
Requiring multi-tasks for even the ordinary
And maybe a need for techno tutor.

So now I have to use both of my phones
In a sort of support each other tandem,
Because while it is easier on my old phone
My new model's success use is quite random.
For whilst I'm catching up a bit with this
And not always having to use both of them,
I still think it may be quite a while before
Laurie two phones can his old one condemn.

--ooOoo--

Prickly Cactus

Now I quite like cactus plants
In fact I do have several myself,
That are displayed about my home
In rooms or on the kitchen shelf.

So they fit in quite attractively
With about thirteen other plants,
That I look after quite religiously
But with the cactus I take a chance,
Of getting myself a painful injury
Because they can be quite dangerous,
Although are pleasant and decorative
When lined up around my house.

For they have very sharp prickles
As an intensive part of their allure,
But best not to be taken in by this
And if you touch them be very sure,
To take care and protect yourself
Or you may recoil from a nasty pain,
That I have suffered myself at times
And not just once but over again.

But at some times you will have to
Change the plants into a bigger pot,
So getting them out and changed over
A simple job it is certainly not,
For I have had to resort to tactics
And ideas almost sent from above
Thus when I need to handle them now
I use a cloth and thick oven glove.

But even these don't always suffice
To avoid pain and protect your hand,
For these cacti can be very spiteful
And that I have come to understand.

So now an arrangement is in place
When my cactus I need to inspect,
Because to ensure all round safety
I treat them with a great respect.

--ooOoo--

Tesco Terry at the Till

Tesco Terry sits uneasy at his till
Ensuring his queue will just stand still,
For the slightest query has him beaten
And leave us realising we'd not eaten,
Before coming into the store and shop
Not knowing we'd be made to stop,
Waiting ages powerless in his queue
As he clearly didn't know what to do.

But his plea to a colleague working near
Seemed to fall deafly and to disappear
As he tried desperately to remain sane
When the colleague muttered "not again!"

So it seemed Terry was not doing well
And by his growing queue you could tell,
That a natural at the checkout he was not
For an impatient queue he had now got.

Though his situation was not helped
By two fussing women making it worse,
With their constant checking of their items
That condemned his checkout like a curse,
Of confused decisions and many mistakes
About which prices on there were correct.
Or more the ones that suited them best
So the cheapest prices they would select.

Thus they'd succeeded in causing chaos
As well as bewildering poor old Terry
Whose shift on the front line checkout till
Had him feeling sick and far from merry.
But none of this concerned our two ladies
Who seemed to think it all a great joke,
Laughing and smiling at me and the queue
Now feeling like giving them a firm poke.

So a few lessons can be learned from this
Particularly for Tesco Terry struggling here,
And to maybe consider another vocation
Or from store checkouts stay well clear.

Meanwhile I'll also be much more aware
When joining lines of women bobbing
About with the items in their baskets
Like an enlarged Batman and Robin,
Stealing everybody's time and patience
Confusing and arguing it all to the end,
As it wasn't just an unhappy Tesco Terry
They'd driven round the sanity bend.

--ooOoo--

Sylvie's Pinnacle

Our Lady Sylvie has reached a pinnacle
Complete with her own special look,
When she volunteered to feature boldly
On the front cover of my latest book.

For Sylvie had been sent a preview
With me in a jester's gown and hat,
That had baubles hanging from it
So she very quickly decided that,
It would be great fun to be so seen
As a smiling photo for one and all,
To view our lovely radio presenter
In not so much a bauble, as a ball.

So proudly on an eye-catching cover
Is a smiling Sylvie Blackmore space,
Alongside three other jolly folks
Surrounding a laughing Laurie's face,
To hopefully attract people to buy
A book full of amusing poetic verse,
Which will certainly lift all moods
To a better place than sad or worse.

Now there is yet another positive in this
Apart from Sylvie being widely shown,
Because every book sold gives to charity
And not all kept by the author alone.
So excellent Help for Heroes will benefit
From a donation from every book sale,
Which with Poet Laurie and Sylvie there
It's likely this fun book won't fail.

--ooOoo--

Curse of the Orange Clad Men

Unlike a silent nocturnal fall of snow
They arrived in the mornings very loud,
Like some demonic brightly clad gang
This baggy overall army, rent-a-crowd.
With white protective hard hats worn
Together with bright orange work gear,
Closing all footpaths and roads down
With a cacophony not good to hear.

Now these orange men aren't political
Although they do invoke strong views,
For they are digging up all our roads
Just whenever and where they choose.
Though even all that isn't the end of it
For two, and three-way traffic lights,
Pop up to cause long frustrated queues
And angry motorist's common sights.

Though pedestrians and residents too
Are also falling foul of this crazy army,
Whose two main disruptive intentions
Are making noise and drive folks barmy.
Because just as you think they've gone
And their patchwork mess is finished,
They will come back to start over again
So hoped-for plans are diminished.

Thus having successfully dug trenches
And caused chaos all over the town,
They repeat the whole process again
Ensuring everyone now wears a frown,
For surely they must get a big bonus
And a fortune for the mess they make.
But meanwhile for all of us innocents
This mob is more than we can take

--ooOoo--

The Silence of The Bears

Ted and Beth have been a bit quiet lately
Basking in the glory of their very own book,
Though I'm always suspicious of any silence
So make sure I always have a good look,
At just what they are now saying or doing
Because they cannot behave for very long,
As mischief, tricks and pranks are habits
Of theirs and the animal gang throng.

So with over thirty teddies and soft animals
That form this collection of lively friends,
Mostly rescued from various charity shops
They make sure that their fun never ends.
Which then makes it quite difficult for me
To keep an eye on any jokes and intents,
Although I'm aware they won't go too far
Knowing I may exclude them from events.

And all the various animals enjoy these
Trips out with me to read and entertain,
Groups and audiences at various venues
So their excitement they can't contain.
But as there are over thirty choices now
I have to ensure that I use a fair rota,
As Ted and Beth always accompany me
So I make sure others get their quota.

Thus now a controlled quiet behaviour
Has settled where the cuddly gang exist,
As they try to be good and then be chosen
So that their turn will not be missed,
For they have also been noticing lately
Other new soft animals joining them all.
Which of course means reduced attention
And less chance of any entertaining hall.

Now all of this may be genuine reasons
Ted and Beth have been quiet and good,
As they welcome new arrivals to the group
Making sure that all rules are understood,
So will have a content community group
And to live together in harmony and calm,
For the bears are enjoying all the company
And make sure none come to any harm.

--ooOoo--

Four Limericks

1

There was a man from Neath
Who lost nearly all his teeth,
And so not to get stuck
He learnt how to suck,
Now he's popular beyond belief.

2

A flirty young woman from Ayr
Loved to make all the men stare,
So she wore her skirts short
Until one had got caught,
And showed off all that was there.

3

There was a fat man from Lahore

Whose clothes can't take any more,

Of the fat he puts on,

But soon he'll be gone

And of that I'm reasonably sure.

4

A very shy girl from Crewe

Wasn't too sure what to do,

So her amorous steed

Then took the lead,

And taught her all that he knew.

--ooOoo--

Bears Greatest Hits

Though Ted and Beth are travelling bears
Sometimes they stay home and rest,
And of all the things they love to do
Listening to music is their best.

Sometimes their Mum will play piano
And they will join in and sing,
Songs about a teddies' picnic place
With lots of goodies they all bring.

Ted and Beth like other songs
Not just about teddy bears,
So among their favourite's is,
About a boy who climbs the stairs.

One Ted and Beth can't work out
Is all about a very strange bear,
Who in gardens walks round and round
And then tickles you under where?

Another song about a famous bear
Whose is known as Super Ted,
But I once heard Beth let slip
She would love him in her bed!

The bears like some pop videos too
With views of the biggest hits,
Elvis, the Beatles and also Queen
And Madonna doing the splits!

But after a while all the songs
Just seem the same refrain,
So they start to get itchy paws
To be off travelling again!

--ooOoo--

Cuddles

Cuddles is a bright, happy monkey
And you can tell that by his smile,
That he appears to wear all day long
So not temporary or for a short while.

Because he's always cheerful and likes
Warm responses he gets from folks,
Due possibly to his bright coloured hair
Almost as flamboyant as his jokes.
That always seem to be well received
By all the people he meets and hugs,
As few can resist his large jolly grin
That on people's heart strings tugs.

So although he still seemed happy
When I found him in a box of toys,
On display at a local charity shop
I think his look is how he employs
His expression on life, good or bad,
Because his situation being for sale,
Wasn't so nice as he tried to show
For he now appeared quite pale.

But I quickly picked him up again
And reassured him he was now saved,
To come with me and the bears family
With the love and laughs he craved.

Thus yet another soft cuddly animal
Joined my bears and animal throng,
And I know he's fine with it all now
For his big smile matched his song.

--ooOoo--

Bella the Robot (Story)

For the Humour section this true story was hilarious for me and involves as title, a robot.

When I visit my daughter in Basingstoke, we regularly go to a large Chinese restaurant that is excellent, but this time they had a new and robotic helper I christened Bella, which is short for its technical name!

Bella would bring your food order to the table but say in robot fashion, "Here I come, and please mind the plates are hot", and also amazingly if a person went near "Excuse me please I'm coming through"!

Wonderful, BUT the show stopper was that it could be programmed to flash and sing Happy Birthday as it brought a complimentary cake to your table. It did this for me, and my daughter has it all on video, AND me, almost for once, lost for words.

Bella the Robot

I first encountered Bella the Robot
At a Chinese restaurant in Basingstoke,
But although I was amused and taken
I could see that it was not a joke.
For this automatic little helper
Was very industrious and careful too,
Serving requested food to customers
And would talk to me and you.

Bella was also sent round to tables
To sing happy birthday wishes as well,
Which made people very appreciative
As by smiling faces you could tell.
But much more than this was the work
Robotic Bella did for all the staff,
Delivering hot plates with great care
While cutting their work load in half.

But our Bella's main amusement for me,
Was her automated voice as she set out
On journey's saying "here I come" now,
Delighting all customers without doubt.
Also politely adding "I am coming past,
So please step out of my way" to us too.
Which nicely puts it into perspective
That of a robot telling us what to do.

Although Basingstoke Bella is not alone
Taylor's in Eastbourne has one as well,
Also providing equal service and fun
Putting us under a sort of robotic spell,
While these cheeky, cheerful robots work
By the side of restaurants serving teams,
To assist, cheer and also amuse us all
As we look at the future it seems.

--ooOoo--

Uni Unicorn

Uni is a mythical fluffy white unicorn
That appears to have a contradictory past.
For a few explanations say it was evil,
But a modern definition of purity will last
Much longer now it has been adopted
As a rainbow decorated symbol of good.
With mentions of fortune and innocence
That are now more widely understood.

But my unicorn is not a real one at all
And has come to join up with my other
Teddies, lions, giraffe, panda and dogs,
Who got separated from their mother,
Or have been left alone in charity shops
Where I recruited them to join me,
As I adopted them for the bears family
That has turned their sadness into glee.

For little Uni, my new cuddly unicorn
Was at the very bottom of a mixed box
Of various toys and other soft animals
That could have then reduced the stocks,
All waiting to be bought and sold there
Thus the temptation was very strong.
But I did recall in time how squashing
And overcrowding the toys was wrong.

But that did not curb my big temptation
To buy and bring more cuddly toys home,
For the bears and their friends reassured me
Being crowded is better than being alone.
So our little white fluffy cuddly unicorn
Has joined the bears and animal friends,
Although aware unicorns had mixed pasts
Ensure that Uni's love and fun never ends.

--ooOoo--

Not Russian About

Our meerkat chap is named Aleksandr Orlov
And that is the correct spelling of his name,
So when he joined us from a charity shop
He fitted in with the others just the same,
As many other discarded orphan rejects did
That joined the teddies and animal crowd.
So they now all enjoy great fun and games
Where sad depression is not allowed.

But Aleksandr did have an initial problem
In that he came from Russia in the past,
Which did cause some early unpopularity
That after his explanation did not last.
As although coming from Russian ties
He had not lived there for many years.
So after the invasion of poor Ukraine
Aleksandr sheds sad, unhappy tears.

But all the teddies and animal family
Won't tolerate any politics in their life,
So now happily accept this meerkat
Without any worries or upsetting strife.
Because most of this animal friend gang
Have some complicated lifetime past,
So are keen to like and readily accept
Uncertainty in their new friend's past.

So our older and distinguished meerkat
Has now happily relaxed and settled in,
And reflects that now the overcrowding
Is annoyingly tight but he can still grin.
But you can see from his carefree stance
That his stomach is just a little bit fat,
But he will only laugh and reassure you
All elders of his species look like that.

--ooOoo--

But Still Not Outshone

Ted & Beth think they have arrived now
Having taken on an understudy pair,
Of an "almost look-alike" teddy couple
But want to say they will still be there,
In the glaring limelight that they love
So won't in any way be stepping aside,
As the thinking is that "Theo and Ami"
Could cover if our stars need to hide.

So for a short time they could rest easy
For with a thirty plus animal gang now,
There is much to do and keep an eye on
And they don't want an unhappy row.

Thus that is how Theo and Lady Ami
Got recruited to occasionally stand in,
To keep good order and contentment
With a calm group not making a din.
For the teddies and various animals
Get excited and out of hand at times,
Often singing and shouting loudly
So would be better if stuck to mimes.

But Ted and Beth can be quite shrewd
Aware having deputies could go wrong,
In as much as they could take it all over
To present their very own act and song.
So Ted and Beth always ensure its them
That will continue to be the main stars,
Because of their hard work undertaken
To be celebrities across the sky to Mars.

So whilst the newly arrived Theo and Ami
Are very cute and give much satisfaction.
Our illustrious pair Ted and Beth both know,
That they are by miles the main attraction.

--ooOoo--

A Cushion for Sylvie

I have written words for Sylvie before
About her stated pinnacle of career,
With also a poem about ears sweating
But now needs a cushion for her rear.

For the queen has had the Jubilee
After seventy years out on her own,
While Sylvie's been around some time
Also sitting on her metaphoric throne,
So she must I think, have some comfort
For that very important part of us all,
As sitting around in just one place
Makes you itch and not look cool.

Thus I present my request again
For a nice regal, comfy sit-upon,
To let Sylvie present in happy peace
And not wish she was up and gone,
For muscle relieving movements
Even if only just a brief little bit.
As there is nothing worse to suffer
Than aches right where you sit.

So this required cushion is crucial
But does not need to cost a mint,
Just enough to help Sylvie sit well
And preside a happy smiling stint,
While knowing that she is now safe
From any creaks or discomfort there,
As with a nice padded cushion in situ,
She can no longer blame the chair.

--ooOoo--

Betting Bears

I caught Ted and Beth out the other day
Watching horse racing and having a flutter,
But I don't think it was going too well
As I heard Ted give out an angry mutter,
That it was all a con and totally fixed
So I guessed then that he hadn't won.
But I don't really mind this too much
As its their money all said and done.

I did notice though that our lovely Beth
Seemed to be far more carefree with it,
Just picking horses with names she liked
Not betting much or worrying one little bit.
While far more intense concentrating Ted
Studied closely on every single horse,
But all that didn't bring him much luck
So he said it was all a fiddle of course.

Now all this seems totally innocuous
And no great problem or concern at all,
Until coming clear Beth kept winning
Which began to drive Ted up the wall.
Because Beth could not resist gloating
That she was far better at it than Ted,
Which really didn't go down very well
As sadly he was losing money instead.

But fear not for our bears in any way
For they really do love each other a lot,
And Beth was more than happy to share
With Ted all the winnings she'd got.

--ooOoo--

Laurie Wilkinson

REFLECTION

Homesick

The snail, tortoise, turtles and such like
All carry about with them their home,
Whilst the vast majority of us going out
Leave our place behind, so we're alone.
Apart from I guess people with a caravan
Mobile home, or perhaps a ladies handbag,
That can contain multiple household things
And many items to make arms sag.

So that's how we can become homesick
If missing where we cut off and relax,
Because we often take things for granted
As we just chill and lay on our backs,
With barely a thought of any negativity
That will never, ever happen to you.
Until something occurs to your home
And then you are lost for what to do.

For it could even be the home itself
Or events and situations in the place,
Should relationships or communications
Break down to leave sadness or disgrace,
As we tend to see our homes as a refuge
Where we can retreat to and be safe,
Thus finding our "little castles" breached
Can soon lead to a loss of faith.

So don't take this sanctuary for granted
Even when we like to travel and roam,
Because it's a very important part of us
And the best road is one going home.

--ooOoo--

A Fair Crack

We like to feel we've had a fair crack
Or even playing field and equal turn,
But life does not always work like that
However much we complain or yearn,
For the chances it appears others had
That you feel were not afforded to you,
As it can then bring about resentment
With discontented, unhappy view.

For if we've tried the same as others
And put in a very similar workload,
It's a completely natural expectation
To be equal distance down the road,
As it would be reasonable to expect
The same reward for effort and energy.
So if sadly that is not quite the case
Protests may be made by you and me.

Although often from the start of life
Privileges and favours may be sent,
For early experiences and environment
Given by benefit of birth clearly meant,
To give a better start and more quality
Over less fortunate who still work hard.
But in an uneven race across our world
They just never have the right card.

For there is now a common outcome
Not always measured by what you do,
But more a background and bearing
That can count as negative against you.
Whilst another form of great injustice
Making us feel bitter and aggrieved,
Is seeing unpleasant people do well
With good folk less awards received.

So make a covenant with yourself
To be pleasantly decent in all you try,
So can live happily in heart and soul
Meeting life with head held high.

--ooOoo--

My Chair

I think most of us have that special place
And that is "my chair" and where I sit,
Because no other seating area at home
Will be as good as that one perfect fit,
Of great comfort and for watching T V
So generally settles you at your ease,
From the cut and thrust of daily life
As your own throne needs no squeeze.

For it has taken the form of your body
Just like a cooking mould for a cake,
To give you that feeling of relaxed joy
And allows each move you make.

So whilst most household sizes vary
On the number of the family group,
Many probably have a favourite perch
If all gathered in the domestic coop.
Though I will venture to be quite bold
In that very few will change their places,
Because however much we do deny it
Most people have favourite spaces.

Now just to add a little more intrigue
Regarding folks living alone and free,
To just go and sit wherever they want
But choose only one special chair to be
Their regular seat without any thought,
When they return home to sit and rest.
For no matter how many free places
Only that "my chair" passes the test.

So I guess I have followed my parents
Who both always sat in the same chair,
To settle and relax in comfortable mode
Without stopping to think or even care.
Therefore I will happily just suggest
Continuing where we put our backside,
When needing to clock off from the day
So I'll relax in "my chair" with pride.

--ooOoo--

All Change

So with diversity now and lots of changes
We really can be excused for not knowing,
Just what, why and who some people are
And wonder if they'll be coming or going.

Because all the freedom of choice on life
Has billowed out to nearly all forms of fun.
As largely with peace and correctness now
Deciding your social group is easily done.

But please don't in any way get me wrong
For I am all for living and letting live,
It's just that sometimes I get confused
About what to say, or how to deal with
Various conglomerations and appearances
That are nowhere near what they seem.
So whilst it is not a major conjecture,
We need to know who's in what team.

Because it seems the more outlandish
Any particular group choose to be,
They can seem extremely defensive
And confronting with you and me,
Which does lead my enquiring mind
To ponder if they are at hearts rest,
While maybe having their inside battle
And hoping they can pass their test.

For happily almost anything goes now
Whether it is natural or perhaps choice,
Just like when we have a ballot election
On who we want to have our voice.

So just settle down and allow all in
Whatever you think about what you saw,
Because if you are tempted to comment
You might unwittingly break the law.

For some situations will baffle and confuse
As we struggle to respond and maybe tell,
Why uncle Fred you've known for years,
Now masquerades as your Auntie Nell?

--ooOoo--

Safe Inside

Loving times, family and friends,
Precious moments shared for you.
But as times can pass and change,
Ensure they're safe in all you do.

For we live snug inside our world,
So don't see much else around.
And very little effects us there,
Thus we sleep secure and sound.

But who can see our inner pain
And take away the hurt and ache?
Of missing people once so close
Nearly every move you make.

So we must count our blessings
And do this every living day.
For memories that we treasure
No one can ever steal away!

--ooOoo--

Are We There Yet?

We often ask if we are there yet?
But where is it that we're going?
For we can't answer one question
If the other we aren't knowing.

As many a hopeful enquirer
Would like everything spelt out,
And what they can soon expect
Because they don't like doubt.

But can we always have the facts
About what's in store for us all?
For it's probably best to carry on
Not knowing if the hammer will fall.

Or maybe it will just be a number
Called out in a lottery game.
But if it's your ball that's drawn
The result will be the same.

So I believe I have the answer now
To the oft asked, are we there yet?
Because I think it means the end
Of the time scale that we get.

For we stagger blindly across the line
Marking the end of our lifetime race.
And praying in the resulting panic,
You arrive with no disgrace.

Thus destination and the getting there
Could be those pearly gates we choose.
So you ask yourself in desperation,
Will your entry they refuse?

--ooOoo--

Lane Strain

The endless narrow leafy lanes
Were graced by overhanging trees too,
And were brought to a sparkling life
When sunlight lanced brightly through,
Those branches and leaves all round
Making the lanes come alive more,
But now also dangerous and restricting
The visibility making drivers unsure.

Because the combination of glaring sun
And rain-spattered, puddle filled road,
Challenged concentration and vision
Like questions from the Highway Code.
So I regularly had to slow down now
To determine just where I was going.
For flickering shadows and sunlight
Can undo the unwary or unknowing.

But apart from the over-riding strain
Of this concentrating and blinking,
Was the natural beauty of the lanes
To appreciate while steadily thinking,
About your speed and the windy road
That seemed to continue for ever.
Which may have been a pleasant scene
If wasn't for the changing weather.

So a sweet and sour journey continued
And seemingly was not having an end,
Battling both relaxing and being alert
For another surprising and sharp bend.

But it is normally right about this time
That I give an appreciation to my car,
For if ever getting confused or even lost
The techno knows just where you are.

--ooOoo--

Back Pass

As I contemplate the world
I must also consider then.
How would I be received,
If I passed this way again?
For unlike the famous saying
We only pass this way one time,
That was more on our whole life
Rather than a local climb.

So back to my conjecture
Of how would I be perceived,
If returning to past haunts
Would I still be well received?
Well certainly I have never
Done anything criminal or dire,
That could be held against me
And cause a greeting to expire.

As I have always tried to live
By not wanting to wear a crown,
And always nice to people going up
I might meet coming down.
And with my other true motto
Possibly the best I ever had,
For if you can't do a good turn,
Then don't do one that's bad.

Thus I really like to think
Happily and with some sway,
That I would be quite welcome
Should I return this way.
For people often mention my laugh
And say I have a ready smile,
But just to be on the safe side
I'll be good for a little while.

--ooOoo--

Lamppost

A lamppost gives a reassuring light
By taking the darkness from the street,
Which gives a nice little area of safety
So that sometimes folks can meet,
Their friends or the odd acquaintance
Before moving on, perhaps to town,
Without any concerns of dark shadows
That make us wear a nervous frown.

For a lamppost is one of those things
Not really noticed until it has gone,
Or possibly it's just having a problem
So that the light doesn't come on.
Which may possibly produce an irony
Maybe making people stop to stare,
If noting a new concerning darkness
When the reassuring light isn't there.

Of course these lamps are very popular
With our four-legged doggy friends,
That will often have a little sprinkle
On a post to mark where territory ends.
Though apparently it could also be a sign
For any canine would be lovers to see,
So their little twinkle on the lamppost
Is a courting call left by their wee.

But our posts are not just functional
As they can be quite decorative too,
With different designs to best fit the area
To make pleasant sights for me and you.
And also depending on how far apart
They can indicate the limits for speed,
Which may save you a stop by police
If they think that there's a need.

Therefore when it is all considered
Our common lamppost has a few roles,
From giving us light and illumination,
To doggy dating and speed controls.

--ooOoo--

The Queen (Story)

After the passing of The Queen in September 2022 I wrote the following poem, but again like many of my poems it has a story behind it. I think it is probably correct to say that virtually everyone was affected at least a little by the passing of our Queen who reigned for 76 years.

I was initially requested to write a poem on the queen by my local area BBC Radio station and to read it out live on air three days later from when she had died, but unfortunately a form of general embargo was made on the media and it wasn't allowed to be read out, not only for me but everybody.

Strangely, as often happens in life, a sort of coincidence occurred in as much as I was asked another three days later if I had written a poem about the queen. Obviously, I had, and so was invited to read it out at the Hailsham vigil for the queen, which was held nationally the Sunday before her funeral the following day, 19th September. Thus I read my poem live in front of about 350 people, who greatly appreciated it.

The Queen

I never got to meet our late Queen
But I understand that many people had,
Although that doesn't really bother me
I do find her tragic passing very sad.
As she seemed to have been our queen
For virtually all of my cognisant life.
Presiding in maternal and caring way,
To guide us along and ease our strife.

So now many moving words of tribute
Are being said about this unique Lady,
Who with majestic manner and dignity
Steered us away from sorrow and shady
Dealings following some leading figures
That Her Majesty side-stepped well,
As controversial relationships emerged
Which deeply upset her, you could tell.

But continuing to serve and put country first
This wonderful woman took it in her stride,
So that now her time is tragically over
We can regard her with an almighty pride.
For certainly we won't see her like again,
As tears flow like from a fractured dam.
So I will now join in with the multitudes
With simple words of "thank you Ma'am".

--ooOoo--

Living Well

If you're thirsty you may go to the well
To quench your thirst with a drink.
And you may do it automatically
Without ever stopping to think,
About how the water got there
Or the need to put something back,
Because the water may soon run dry
If the well is allowed to crack.

For in our world little comes for free
Although plenty will live for this,
By taking out everything they can
And giving help requests a miss.
For they are too busy taking all
It's possible to get lazy hands upon,
Ensuring when it's payback time
They'll be well and truly gone.

So for us in a concerned majority
Is the need take care of our well
And other gifts passed on to us,
As they are not ours to waste or sell.
When the sacrifice of many others
Gave them up without a cost,
Only a big responsibility of trust
To see they are never lost.

Thus this commitment is now ours
To appreciate and protect this wealth,
Of the things we may take for granted
All the time they're in good health.
But just a little thought and effort
Will see our gifts all safely supplied,
And to know our drinking well is flowing
Will meet our wish after we've died.

--ooOoo--

Hospitalisation

We know an underfunded NHS is creaking
So I did wonder a bit what I would find,
When having to be rushed into hospital
But it wasn't the main thing on my mind.
For I was in severe agony and worrying
Just what was causing my intense pain,
But on being met by an emergency doctor
I got a reassured confidence back again.

For I was soon to be looked after very well
And treated in a valued and dignified way,
Which embraced all involvements from staff
Not seemingly to falter or even sway,
From a totally caring, committed approach
And camaraderie gallows humour for events,
Testing, saddening and shredding stout hearts
But never diminished any of their intents.

Thus as I considered this new world for me
For I had never been in hospital before,
I was impressed by positivity and hard work
Of various team grades giving all and more,
That could be reasonably asked of them now
With staff shortages and pressure of work,
From budget cuts and paltry wage rises
Grating on levels of duty they do not shirk.

So let us not treat our NHS with impunity
Or overuse the services unless we have to,
For these overcrowded committed areas
Normally have more than enough to do.
Therefore we must do our very level best
And stay sensible and use common sense,
To be healthy and look after ourselves
So pressure on NHS is not so immense.

--ooOoo--

Inner Depths

I have a dark invader in me
Who tries to get into my soul,
I fight him off to keep him out
But he buries down like a mole.
So what actually is this menace?
I can't tell you as I'm not sure,
For he rarely comes to meet me
But into an abyss tries to lure.

For even the very brightest heart
Will have some darker days,
And it's at these very moments
The invader stalks and preys.
Because that is our weak link
When even fleeting doubts are cast,
As when down, problems are larger
So must be resisted until passed.

But I have an inner strength
Gained by having seen the worst
That life will throw at us,
And feeling my heart would burst.
So I now know that if I wait,
Without succumbing to the pain
Of that dour and depressive spell
My resistance I will regain.

Thus deep down inside my being
A battle is often fought,
Between my courage and dark invader
Though you may have no thought,
That all this is going on
And that I may be losing for a while,
Because I will always look the same
And take refuge behind my smile.

--ooOoo--

The Funny Man

I met him at the bar in a local hotel
Where he was sharing jokes with staff,
But he told me he was always funny
And renowned for making folks laugh.
Now I was very surprised to hear this
For we had literally only just met,
And it struck me it was huge self-praise
To someone who he didn't know yet.

But he was quite insistent with his line
Of how popular and known he was now,
So I continued to be quietly bemused
In the face of his very confident vow,
Of being an outstanding mister popular
Alongside his apparent hilarious wit.
For it was all the total opposite with me
As I wasn't liking him one little bit.

Because I was brought up with values
About not laughing at your own jokes,
Or singing high praises about yourself
Amid fears of bad reactions it provokes.
But this had clearly passed our man by
For his self-importance, was over the top,
And although he knew nothing about me
His self-trumpet blowing did not stop.

So apart from going to the same meeting
The self-acclaimed star did not know me,
Or anything that I had achieved or did
But I realised he would not want to see,
Anything people had done successfully
For he clearly thought he was the best.
But sadly with myself and many others
He really was going to fail this test.

Thus any claimed hilarity or achievements
Were firmly put into a more modest space,
So he eventually did soon quieten down
Deflated, and with a surprised loss of face.

--ooOoo--

Where?

Where have all my years gone
And can I please get them back?
I promise that I won't waste them
For I never let sad times stack
Up too highly in my world,
In those years of mine now past.
And I nearly always enjoyed myself
I guess why time went so fast.

So where have those years gone
Along with so many great days?
For I can still vividly remember
The songs and music that plays,
Like a magical memory jukebox
Rewinding much love and fun,
As they bring back situations
Where all was said and done.

Oh I can recall so many people
Sadly though some have gone,
Though their days are remembered
When they danced and faces shone,
From disco lights and silhouettes
Or maybe it was too much drink.
But that was in the distant past
Which makes me stop to think,
Just where have my years gone?
For it doesn't seem that long,
When my features were pristine
Like some newly written song.

Now as I look very fondly back
Over all those years I've had,
And people met and places seen
With more happier days than sad,
I feel my lifetime has stretched
Across many a stunning sunset,
But I hope for more to come
As I'm not ready to go just yet!

--ooOoo--

Past Echoes

There is a teardrop on the table
From the whispers of the past,
For all the dreams and plans
That somehow did not last.

Despite all, you've emerged now
Out from those mists of time,
Saw the rivers that contained you
And the hills you could not climb.

So you made your way regardless
Of the pitfalls and the traps,
And settled in your castle
With scarce a dip or lapse.

Maybe your destiny is different
From what you'd hoped it would be,
But looking back from now
At that time you could not see
Without the gift of foresight
Just how everything would end.
So thoughts of could've, should have
Are now just scars to mend.

Of course it could be different
From how it's all turned out,
Knowing then just what would happen
We would succeed without a doubt.
But life never is that simple
When the answers can be seen,
So we would make new errors
After the old ones we redeem.

--ooOoo--

Young Old Men

Some blokes stay like young old men
Demonstrating it for the world to see,
But others will old young men remain
And I decided that would not be me,
Because whilst health can play a part
A lot of little things are down to you,
Such as attitude, manner or your look
Which includes what you say or do.

Because I also believe if you are happy
In both your heart and in your head,
You've made a covenant with yourself
And so no more needs to be said,

For most things are really quite simple
Such as clean, smart modern clothes,
Along with a pride in your appearance
To make you more presentable than those
Who take very little time or attention
About how they're involved and look,
Or ensure to be up dated and interested
And not seem like an old dusty book.

Now I can hear some cynics muttering
About mutton dressing up as lamb,
But if your presentation is appropriate
There is no need to look a sham.
For if you care about personal hygiene
Alongside awareness that you know,
It's important to look after yourself
And not just let yourself go.

For some old young men have done that
And seem much older than their years,
To wonder why they're unfit and unhealthy
From no exercise and too many beers.

Although nothing is wrong with drinking
Provided those pounds are not piled on,
But it may not be just old looks you have
A now you very soon could be gone,
So no more to be inert and overindulge
Or have to worry about being smart.
Because when it's far too late now,
You'll wish you made a better start.

--ooOoo--

TRAGEDY

Nudged Awake

Steady, steady Laurie boy go carefully
And don't let your controversy show,
But oh why ever not I then debated,
As without that people won't know,
Your views and opinions on our life
That maybe they'd not thought about,
So yeah I'll lay it clearly on the line
Possibly ending a thinking drought.

Because some people do like to read
Or watch the more outspoken people,
As they like to have some cut and thrust
To lift them high as a church steeple.
For the world would seem quite dull
If nobody will dare to cause a fuss,
So that again totally suits me now
When I am often as subtle as a bus.

But I'm not always like this now
Unlike some folk with regular scowl,
Who will cynically comment on all
That to them seems unhappily foul.
For it appears they have a deep regret
Of anything they don't have or can't do,
Thus will spit out very spiteful words
With a sad jealousy for me or you.

So I believe my rarer controversies
May illuminate or even bring a smile,
To those dour and deprecatory folk
Needing something brighter for a while,
For my given one-line catchy words
Can cause some amusement and thought,
Especially more for those among us
That are down in the doldrums caught.

--ooOoo--

A First Time

The soft hand touching my stomach
Made me cry out in agonising pain,
And the continuing examination
Caused me to call out once again.

For it was clear from investigations
That really didn't need too long,
As chronic pain and tender reactions
Proved something was very wrong.
Because I had never had this before
Making me have to attend at A and E,
With a two-day long stabbing agony
That seemed to be crucifying me.

But I soon got great help and attention
With pain relief and antibiotics too,
Put into me by two intravenous drips
And a planned scan to see what to do,
With my very sore and swollen stomach
And gall bladder that was highly infected,
Which was apparently inflamed as well
Thus a big shock and totally unexpected.

So for the very first time in all my years
I was admitted to hospital for four days,
With the possibility of an operation too
If my scan showed any signs or displays,
That my gall bladder needed removing
But at this moment that is all on hold,
Awaiting further investigations and tests
Before the decision on that I am told.

So an extremely weak and tired yours truly
Was discharged back to my home alone,
By an extremely helpful red cross charity
Who came to help as I lived on my own.
That was greatly appreciated and helpful
As I was barely even as strong as a kitten,
Which was a new and surprising situation
For I had never before been this smitten,
Or laid low by illness and hospital stay
Needed to cure my infection and pain,
As I wait for news on possible operation
To avoid any hospitalisation again.

--ooOoo--

Bullies in War

Calculatingly the great Russian bear
Has started another cruel war again,
Invading the close little Ukraine's border
For greater power, greed and sick gain,
Which sent reverberations round the world
In the shapes of economy, food and fear,
And also brings us closer to nuclear war
We hoped would never again come near.

So for months now the world watched on
At T V reports of terror, torture and killing,
Of quiet, ordinary people now condemned
To be reluctant spectators of bullies instilling,
Horror to poor, simple and peaceful folks
Desperately clinging on to their past life.
As close families are all torn apart, or worse
On the back of enforced terror and strife.

But freedom is a precious commodity
And has been bravely fought for before,
So a determined Ukraine, army and people
Are valiantly fighting back to shut the door,
On ignorant tyrants oblivious or just ignoring
The condemnation of all the world at large.
But should they ever consider that at all
Maybe they will in the next failed charge.

Thus we all hold our breath in sympathy
For the suffering of an occupied Ukraine,
Whilst having to dig deeper in our pockets
To pay for the financial costs of war again.
But there is no price you can ever place
On the horrors, wounds or many lives taken
As atrocities and sufferings continue daily,
Upon a people feeling lost and forsaken.

So share thoughts and pity for Ukraine
And pay the spiralling costs without fuss.
For however much frustrated anger it causes,
We should feel lucky that its them, not us.

--ooOoo--

And Still the Wind

But that is a classic contradiction
For the wind is never still or calm,
With unpredictable times and power
Apart from motions of a wind farm.

For wind can exist as a pleasant breeze
Or unleash gale force gusts of power,
Which can cause untold damage and ruin
If it should continue for hour after hour,
That on frightening occasions is the case
With trees uprooted, chaos and lives lost.
For with severe hurricanes and storms
We can often only just count the cost.

Therefore we must take heed and care
If Mother Nature shows a strong effect,
By demonstrating power and maelstroms
Inflicting fear with everything wrecked.

Thus helplessly and feeling very humble
Us mere mortals must just stand and see
How insignificantly puny we are at times,
Confronted by forces that won't let us be.
Or take refuge and retreat back to science
And inventions that make us feel so good.
But as spectators of unfolding disaster,
Our limited abilities become understood.

Yet still the wind can prevail and teach
A human race sometimes above its station
In the pecking order of nature's universe,
With unlearned lessons and education.

--ooOoo--

Blanket

You sort of accepted all the dampness
But tonight there was a coldness too,
So you snuggled up into your blanket
For it was now all that you could do,
As you surveyed the mass devastation
That prevailed everywhere around.
So you scuttled about almost ant like,
Over disputed bloodstained ground.

Which remained a gruesome stalemate
After earlier failed hopeful assaults,
That had just led to sickening carnage
As generals argued over who's faults,
Had reduced flowers of a generation
To exist in a drowning mud soaked hell,
Fighting to eke their miserable life out
And dodge the next incoming shell.

Thus the new recruit watched me closely
Eyes bewildered and etched with fear,
As each new and thunderous explosion
Caused cascading craters far and near,
While he too struggled with discomfort
Battling to keep his body alive and warm,
And trying to ignore grenades and bullets
Buzzing like a demented bees swarm.

So I helped him sort out his big blanket
And showed the best way without doubt,
For he nodded, grinned and thanked me
Just as an enemy sniper took him out.

--ooOoo--

Goodbyes

Some goodbyes are happy, others are not
I guess it depends on the thoughts you've got,
That have made you decide to up and go
Maybe to a future you can't possibly know,
If it will prove to be the very best thing
And happy and glorious times will bring.
But in life we must risk such brave bets
Or perhaps be condemned to sad regrets.

So perhaps happy goodbyes are easier
As they mostly appear to fall into place,
Of times that seem right for departures
Without need for upset or any disgrace.
Although of course there may be sadness
With the leaving and closing of a door.
But such times can occur quite naturally
Without any feelings of a civil war.

Sadly in the case of tougher goodbyes
There can be bad blood and acrimony,
And deep feelings of injustice or anger
If involving people like you and me.
For in our world things can change
Not always chosen, or for the best,
Which can cause disputes with others
And heartaches setting us all a test.

Thus preferred on our road of life
Is trying to steer a neutral route,
To avoid upsets bringing us down
But that option doesn't always suit,
As while not always our decisions
Rows happen or relationships end,
To disrupt our sleep and thoughts
Of goodbye to a partner or friend.

--ooOoo--

Behind Me?

I guess I was just too busy being unwell
And in such severe pain to stop and think,
For all my concerns and fears were such
That I couldn't concentrate or even blink,
Over what other events were occurring
Apart from me needing a hospital bed.
Which was a new cardinal shock for me,
To contemplate anything else instead.

For I do now recall a doctor saying
How I was a very seriously ill case,
So at that time it didn't register much
I might be going to that other place,
From which there is no coming back
Or even have much choice it seems.
So I determined to get well and recover
And not dwell on nightmarish dreams.

But having largely all recovered now
Only needing to get my strength back,
I have reflected on my recent situation
With updated thoughts that now stack,
Across my mind as I try to process it all
Or how it may have alternately turned out.
Because it had given me a massive shock
And deep concerns without a doubt.

So I have now come to this conclusion
That I might not have heard the knock,
Upon my metaphoric door for me
To give me that huge ultimate shock,
As I believe now my unwanted visitor
Was the fearsome, dreaded reaper grim,
Deciding that he would take his chance
To force me to go away with him.

Thus I now count even more blessings
And consider I had a very lucky escape,
For I was far too ill to know or be aware
He sought to take me off under his cape.
So I survived to live on many more days
Much to that grim characters great regret.
For though he wanted me for his dead army,
I'm nowhere near ready to go just yet.

--ooOoo--

Not the Kids (Story)

The title really says what this is about, but like many of my poems, it's never quite that simple until you've read it all.

Regretfully, many marriages and relationships of couples end in an acrimonious manner, and often with any children involved caught in the middle and seeing the arguments of their parents. This is rarely easy for them to deal with, so these are difficult times for all involved.

Even more regretful, however, is the frequent selfish attitude to children involved who often become like prizes in obscene tugs of war, so my poem starts with this, but following a glut of horrendous incidents at my time of writing, descends into absolute horror.

This is tragically explained when various parents kidnap or go on to kill the children, with sometimes their recent partner as well, so the children are slain as in "if I cannot have them, neither can you" attitude, thus I offer my poem, Not the Kids!

Not The Kids

Human nature will always tempt and decree
The making of couples to want to be three,
Or not exactly three, more move onto another
Who seems nicer, and a much better lover.
So all that has been built is likely to fall
For a lust temptation will now risk it all.

But please don't forget about your little one's
Who may feel their lives are buried under tons,
Of retribution, bile and a new angry world
After protective guardians become unfurled,
From secure, loving and happy family state
To a selfish feud of retribution and hate.

So now that's a very sad and heavy load
For any young child to feel and see,
When vows are forgotten and anger rules
Allowing the release of a vindictive spree,
Where children become like chess pieces
Moved around or used to hurt the other,
Now totally forgetting their commitment
To be a loving, caring father or mother.

Because often if one parent feels aggrieved
They may take action beyond any control,
And take dangerous risks with the children
With many cruel acts from heart and soul.

For your kids can't be in way to blame
If love has gone and someone cheated,
So leave young innocents out of it
If revenge passions become overheated.

Because too many cases have occurred
When retribution of jealous rage ensue,
And children are taken or even killed
In an "if I can't have them, nor will you".

For human behaviour can sink to depths
Of shame that you cannot ever atone,
So however angry or upset you are
Please leave your children alone.

--ooOoo--

Inner Tears

I have heard that when you cry
Tears are words hearts can't express,
But whatever reason for their visit
It can be a sign of great distress.

Of course there are tears of joy
And some of laughter in a form,
But none can seem as heart-rending
As anguish riding out a storm.

Tears of grief or frustration perhaps
Are streaming down your face,
You should not be ashamed of this
As it really is no disgrace.
For those who cry are often caring
And so let their passions free,
Unlike blank faced stone hearts
That other people's woe can't see.

We can cry at the world's sadness
Or what it has all done to us,
So some will weep out openly
Others cry with much less fuss.
But however you shed your tears
When pain's too much to bear,
It just proves you have empathy
And that you do, really care.

So pucker up, let yourself go
Express emotions and your views,
For if you cannot manage this
You live a life that has no clues.

--ooOoo--

True or False

How did so much time creep up on me
And just where did all the years go,
Because however much I rack my brain
I have to accept that I just don't know,
How I've arrived at this moment in time
Which has made me stop and think,
Over my lifetime and various events
That seemed to pass in a mere blink.

Because when I look back at my time
I'm pleased and happy I did so much,
So then smile with a warm glow inside
Before realising that I must now clutch
Dearly at the time I may have left
As maybe there won't be many years,
For new memories and experiences
With again more laughs than tears.

So is it true or false when looking back
To count our blessings, time and fun,
For considering and appraising it all
You realise most of your race has run,
As there are only so many allocated years
Of varying times for the human race,
With some only allowed short-terms
Others with poor health to embrace.

Thus I'm saying don't get me wrong
For I am a happy and lucky man,
Who has had, and is still living now
The very best life anyone can.

So please indulge my little moments
Which I am sure come to us all,
As we confront our autumn time
Knowing winter can make us fall,
To depart then from this mortal coil
Leaving just our legacies to be seen,
And decide if for us it was true or false
That our time was all it could've been.

--ooOoo--

One in Three

Love and laughter may sprinkle around
With no real problems for you and me,
But we must always be aware of the fate
That will befall every one in three.

For our lives can change in a trice
When the world sends us a test,
To deal with tragedy, failure or loss
When we are forced to do our best,
To keep our chins up and smile
And face the world with fragile pride,
That may fool many, and maybe you
Until you realise you're dying inside.

As a blackness so dark falls all over you
With no pinprick of light in your pit,
So you blunder about and don't even try
Whilst every sinew begs you to quit,
And perhaps shuffle off this mortal coil
That right now seems most appealing,
For even if you do try to fight back
You're overwhelmed by a darkest feeling.

Where has all this come from you ask?
But in truth you may never know,
How you are reduced to anxiety tears
And constant feelings of death and woe,
That will affect many now in their lives
As if have swallowed a depressive pill,
For you have become one in the three
Who learn the trauma to be mentally ill.

--ooOoo--

Lessons to be Learnt

Your country needs you the posters said
And you can fight beside your chums,
So off they went to the war in France
And said goodbye to girls and mums.

Very ordinary chaps, not heroes yet
Were all excited, feeling hearts soar,
Marching off to their great adventure
To win a war that will end all war.

Well that was the propaganda then
And may even have been said in fear,
For sadly that was not to happen
At any time after, or in a future year.
Because the unprecedented bloodbath
Caused mass suffering and deprivation,
As world war one's attrition dragged on
With atrocities that stunned a nation.

So men who were totally unprepared
Witnessed sights that shouldn't be seen,
Like petrified men drowning in mud,
Gassed, or blown up in deaths obscene.
Thus casualty figures hardly believable
Rose as the slaughter went on unabated.
For that final push was regularly tried
On wasted, bloody ground not sated.

With thousands of men mowed down
Strewn in agony or a hideous death,
Many crucified across the barbed wire
As devils' disciples gasped for breath,
While their evil work was continued
But performed by unknowing men,
Who had only answered a patriotic call
That took them to hell there and then.

And so agonising slaughter continued
By new weaponry invented to kill,
Flowers of a generation sent to solve
Arguments that war never will.

--ooOoo--

Grave Decision

There is no one at home
Because the door is locked.
No way in there for you
But are you really shocked?

Many times you tried to call
The phone just kept on ringing.
Mobile goes to answer phone,
No joy will that be bringing.

Of course you could send a text
She will never fail to see,
But still you get no reply
How obvious can it be?
You are in a contact ban
No interest in what you stutter,
It's far too late for you now
Whatever things you mutter!

Hasty words and decisions made
Without engaging the brain,
You can't go back and change it
So won't be the same again.

It's done then now you say
If that is how it lies,
You don't want a big drama
But you never said goodbyes.
Now everything is up in the air,
No clue to how it stands.
Though for you the music's gone,
No choir or marching bands.
Hasty words and decisions made
Without engaging the brain,
You can't go back and change it
So it won't be the same again.

It is said that wounds heal,
And every war will end.
But you know it's over now,
However much you pretend!

--ooOoo--

Home Alone

The sound from the radio filled the air
And is on mostly to break the silence,
That can prevail, if welcome or not
Or if feelings are relaxed or tense.

For on occasions silence can be loud
And then seem to penetrate the soul,
Reducing both the stoic and strongest
To a dark, depressing downward roll,

But at other times the quiet is welcome
Like sight a beautiful mountain spring,
And when a sweet happy solitude reigns
With lovely memories that it can bring.

Therefore we can see a contradiction
Between sweet silence or dark mind,
That may still creep up and take you
From any contentment that you find.
Because moods vary on a daily basis
About your life and just what you do.
Thus be prepared to get caught out
If any loneliness descends on you.

So now I always count my blessings
With mostly having an upbeat stance,
And that any small joke or happiness
Can make me want to sing and dance.
Although I guard against those times
When uncertain feelings seek us out,
Like finding that everything indoors
Is just exactly as when you went out.

Thus we must make our covenant
About how we will act and feel,
Because life can come swinging in
With depressions that may try to steal,
Moments that we thought were safe
Protected behind both lock and key.
For I can now fully describe this
As it often tries to disturb me.

--ooOoo--

An Inside Job

On a night of non stirring air
With anonymous perfection,
That's the time to sit and deal
With deeds that need correction.

For any self-doubt or sorrow
And a pain that never goes,
Has to be sorted, or put right,
Or it like a cancer grows.

But running away or hiding
Was not the way to solve,
Problems hid, or still denied
Should that be your resolve.

How could you ever run away
Or leave others all deceived?
When you know for certain sure
You will never be believed.

So best for heartfelt honesty
On that night of non stirring air,
With its anonymous perfection
You must be forced to dare,
To tear off all that armour
Which protects the unseen you,
And come to terms with feelings
That on your inside grew!

--ooOoo--

Appendix

Kind compliments and feedback to me on my poetry increases as I continue to write and produce more books, number twelve now, but it still recounts that many people like to work out the meanings of my poems for themselves, or even attach their own personal experiences and thoughts as they resonate with them.

I think that is truly wonderful, AND for other folks who like to seek my reasons and explanations for my poems, please review my comments below.

As I tend to write spontaneously and often on subjects that have had an emotional impact on me, I will mostly "nail my thoughts in", so, most of the themes should be quite clear or self-explanatory.

That said, the poems listed in this appendix below are the less obvious topics and thoughts. Please feel free to attach any personalisation or special meaning that they have for you individually, I will feel really honoured if you do!

Beam of Love:
That maybe dreams can come true.

Trinket:
Very important possessions are not always dear and expensive.

Are We There Yet?:
My taken on that oh too often asked question.

A Cushion for Sylvie:
My joking with Sylvie Blackmore live on air about The BBC not providing her with a comfy cushion to sit on.

My Chair:
That nearly everybody seems to have their favourite chair they must sit in.

All Change:
On idealistic issues and thoughts about gender, identification and sex change.

Safe Inside:
Appreciate who and what you have, while you have it, and before it has gone.

Lane Strain:
Another warning for drivers in face of changing weather and driving conditions.

Living Well:
Look after all we have, and to preserve the world for future generations.

Inner Depths:
That depressing thoughts will strike more when we are struggling, and that many people will be oblivious of fights within others.

The Funny Man:
About my first meeting with a ludicrously self-praising and conceited man who truly believed he was the wittiest and star of life, but clearly wasn't.

Past Echoes:
On looking back over life and identifying changes made and successes you had.

Young Old Men:
Describing that some people have young approaches to life, whilst others are drab and dire whilst still young.

Nudged Awake:
Making your thoughts known in appropriate or amusing manner.

Bullies of War:
My condemnation of Russian invasion of Ukraine February 2022.

And Still the Wind:
On however damaging and unpleasant the wind is and our dislike of it, we have no control over it.

Blanket:
Snapshot of the dire World War One trench life and trench war generally.

Goodbyes:
My descriptions of amicable and sometimes difficult farewells or leaving.

Not The Kids:
That children should not be dragged into tempestuous relationship endings.

Inner Tears:

A recent competition winner for me about releasing of emotions.

True or False:

Strong thoughts about reflection of stages of our life, but particularly older years, and how we deal or dealt with it all.

Home Alone:

On recognising and coming to terms with living alone and maybe loneliness.

An Inside Job:

About resolving and not ignoring or being in denial of any concerns.

Laurie Wilkinson

More?

I hope that you enjoyed this book
For I tried to pack lots in,
With various themes in sections
So you can choose where to begin,
And take yourself on journeys
Or if you wished to, just remain.
For I have other books out now,
Thus you can have it all again.

With poems to make you romantic
And some verses if you feel deep.
Others will make you look back on life,
Even smile when you go to sleep.

Of course Ted and Beth will feature
I can hardly leave them out.
As surely they'll have new adventures,
Well of this I have no doubt!
And I will have new observations
I glean from scanning life's tree.
Take care then you are not included
When I write down what I see.

So please look at my other books
And support "Help for Heroes" too,
For all my sales donate to them
From my poems I write for you.

You can get books from my website online

And to message me direct will be fine.
With every contact listed below
Including all that you need to know,
To search for me on the Amazon club
Or just come and find me down the pub!

My other books are: -
Poetic Views of Life
MORe Poetic Views of Life
Reviews of Life in Verse
Life Scene in Verse
Life Presented in Verse
Poet Reveals All
Poet Reflects Your World
Our World in Verse
Laurie's Bundle of Poetic Humour
Tea for Two: Poetic Antics of Ted & Beth

My contacts: -
Email = lw1800@hotmail.co.uk
Amazon authors page= Laurie Wilkinson
Facebook page = The Psychy Poet Laurie
Wilkinson
Facebook page =Ted n Beth of Laurie the Poet
Website = www.lauriewilkinson.com

Printed in Great Britain
by Amazon

18649609R00088